COVID CHURCH

The Before & After Church (BAC)
Attendance Growth Idea

I   **Increase Attendance**

D   **Drive Online Engagement**

E   **Equip Attendees to Invite Others**

A   **Advance Like Never Before**

Marnie Swedberg

COVID Church:
The Before & After Church (BAC)
Attendance Growth Idea

Copyright 2020
by Marnie Swedberg
https://www.Marnie.com

Published in the United States of America.

No part of this book may be used or reproduced in any manner whatsoever without written permission except in the case of brief quotations embodied in critical articles and reviews.

For more information contact:
Gifts of Encouragement, Inc.
3773 Howard Hughes Parkway, 500 S
Las Vegas, NV 89169-0949
877-77-HOW-TO
877-774-6986
Info@Marnie.com
http://www.Marnie.com.

Swedberg, Marnie.
COVID Church:
The Before & After Church (BAC)
Attendance Growth Idea
p. cm.
ISBN 978-0-9829935-7-6
1. Church Growth. 2. Church Leadership
I. Title: COVID Church
First Edition/Book: 2020

TABLE OF CONTENTS

— **5** ASSESSMENT: EVALUATE YOUR CURRENT SITUATION

— **7** CONVERSATION VS. OBSERVATION

— **10** TWO UNIQUE CONGREGATIONS

4

12 US VS. THEM VERSION 2020

17 GOOGLE MEETS FOR COVID CHURCHES

22 BRING 'EM B.A.C. (BEFORE & AFTER CHURCH)

26 TYPES OF ONLINE OPPORTUNITIES TO OFFER

29 30-SECONDS TO SUCCESS

34 LOOKING BEHIND TO PLAN AHEAD

38 APPENDIX I: THE 5WS

41 APPENDIX II: INSIGHTS FROM SUCCESSFUL ROOM HOSTS

45 ABOUT THE AUTHOR

COPYRIGHT 2020 © WWW.MARNIE.COM

Evaluate Your Current Situation

Assessment

Use this simple assessment to find out if this idea is right for your congregation to help your stay-at-home folks feel more like they are still on your radar and a vital part of their church family.

It's no surprise that pastors and church leaders are finding it difficult to connect with their at-home congregations. It might come as a surprise to discover you've been unintentionally under-serving your at-home saints. It follows that this season of vulnerability has led to church hopping, or worse, the giving up of church attendance altogether.

Fill in the blanks on the chart on the next page to identify if extra action is required by your team. Enter the number of one-on-one conversations you've recently had with attendees in the middle column. Compare those numbers to the numbers in column three.

Your Engagements	Your 1-on-1 Interactions On-Premise	Your 1-on-1 Interactions with Those at Home
This Past Sunday	# _____	# _____
Last Week (Mon-Sat)	# _____	# _____
The Sunday Before	# _____	# _____

SUGGESTION: Share this assessment with your staff. Repeat as needed. Keep records as a reminder and for encouragement.

chapter 1
CONVERSATION VS. OBSERVATION

Let's review the timeline.

- In Phase I of COVID-19, you were required to move your entire church online.
- Phase II saw you reopen, partially.
- Now in Phase III, you're pastoring two congregations: one online and the other on-premise.

chapter 1
CONVERSATION VS. OBSERVATION

While your on-premise congregation has significantly moved past the initial shock of the coronavirus pandemic, your "stuck at home" congregation is still in the thick of a precautionary lifestyle.

Some stay home out of fear. Others stay home due to godly wisdom re: high-risk vulnerabilities for themselves or a family member. A final group is using the pandemic as an excuse for non-attendance.

All of them feel like outsiders looking in due to the huge disparity between attending online and on-premise.

Review the chart on the following page for further clarification.

Chapter 1
CONVERSATION VS. OBSERVATION

ON PREMISE	ONLINE
Leave the house with anticipation.	Boot up the computer.
Arrive, park, walk and greet as you go.	
Greet and be greeted in the foyer.	
Find a seat and converse with neighbors.	
Enjoy the service, get lost in the Spirit, singing loudly, and be present in the moment.	Watch and do your best to sing along despite feeling self-conscious. Try to stay focused while being distracted by other online options.
Receive prayer at the altar if needed.	
Greet others on your way out.	
Arrive home two or more hours later or go out for lunch with friends.	Begin to do something else one minute later.

COPYRIGHT 2020 © WWW.MARNIE.COM

Chapter 2
TWO UNIQUE CONGREGATIONS

One of your roles, as pastor, is to facilitate fellowship between all your believers. This resource was created to support you as you help the lonely and alienated to feel included instead of invisible.

The goal is conversation versus simple observation.

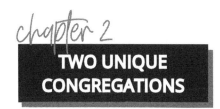

Chapter 2
TWO UNIQUE CONGREGATIONS

Now is the time to embrace a proactive response, because more challenges are on the way.

- Flu season is here resulting in a second wave of vulnerability.
- We're facing social unrest.
- Families and businesses are facing financial struggles.
- We are experiencing a hostile election environment.

The goal of a COVID-sensitive response is to engage, protect and equip our vulnerable, online congregations.

It is imperative we do not just "wait to see" how things turn out. We need to act quickly.

chapter 3
US VS. THEM VERSION 2020

We see it in society and in our newly separated COVID-churches of 2020: It's a growing sense of "us vs. them."

When COVID-19 first struck, all of us were forced to "shelter in place," meaning everyone was stuck at home. For the sake of our vulnerable populations, we accepted that restriction.

US VS. THEM
VERSION 2020

But now, as some people get to go to the building while the rest stay tucked away at home, there is an undercurrent of unrest bubbling to the surface.

Grief counselors know that deep-seated, residual feelings from wounds of the past meld with current sadness to create a new layer of grief.

Our current season of segregation has revealed past hurts and other emotions related to feeling left out or overlooked.

The "selective" confinement of some of your congregation (which is in no way your fault) has the potential to multiply emotional strain, causing mild to major negative reactions, which can morph into full-blown discontent. Feelings of inequity or injustice tend to be directed toward any source of a perceived wrong.

We're seeing it on the streets, we're seeing it in families, and now we're seeing it in the housebound church.

chapter 3
US VS. THEM VERSION 2020

In the women's ministries where I spend most of my time, gals have been verbalizing sentiments such as, "I just don't feel like I belong anymore," or "I'm so lonely. At least you guys get to see each other." Another sentiment we've heard goes like this, "I'm on the outside looking in. I'm not a part of what's happening," or "I don't feel as if I'm needed, or even noticed."

These painful sentiments have triggered the beginning of the corrosion of the online church. Saints are either abandoning their home churches (to check out mega churches online), or they're simply not bothering to watch anywhere, "at least for a while."

Here's what they're saying:

> "We're taking a break," or "It's not like real church," or "I'm tired of just watching," or "What does it matter? No one misses me."

One faithful saint, in a moment of honest reflection, said it like this:

US VS. THEM VERSION 2020

"I feel guilty saying this, but here's what I'm thinking. 'I'm still attending online and sending in my tithes and offerings, but I have no idea how the money is being used. Are the pastors visiting or calling people? Are the youth pastors touching base with the kids who can't attend? Are there small groups going on?'"

Pastor, it's as if you've given birth to a second child-an online church. Instead of the older child (the on-premise church) experiencing sibling rivalry, it's the baby, your newborn online church, that is screaming for attention.

This congregation is isolated and starving for interaction.

They're lonely, alienated and afraid of the future.

Just three months ago you were applauded for taking your ministry online. Now is appears that very action has morphed into a source of discontentment and division.

chapter 3
US VS. THEM VERSION 2020

The great news is that there is an easy solution at hand. The idea is called Before and After Church (BAC) online chat rooms.

chapter 4
GOOGLE MEETS FOR COVID CHURCHES

Here are some established facts:

- Attending church in person requires health, faith, or both. At-risk individuals may not have the option of attending church yet, or for quite some time to come.

chapter 4
GOOGLE MEETS FOR COVID CHURCHES

- Watching online offers observation but no conversation.
- For many people, attending an online chat room, such as Zoom, can be intimidating.

Allow me to introduce you to Google Meets as a solution for Before and After Church (BAC) engagement. Google Meets can replicate our beloved foyer-style conversation experience, as even the most technology-phobic people can participate with ease.

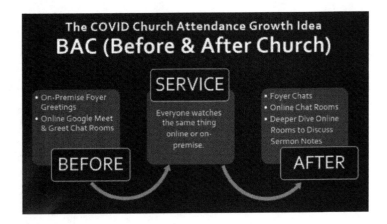

GOOGLE MEETS FOR COVID CHURCHES

Unlike Zoom and other online group meeting platforms (which are ideal for computer-savvy saints), Google Meets attracts and retains non-techy attendees and potential small group leaders who've otherwise felt intimidated.

Google Meets makes it simple for everyone to participate.

Watch these short tutorials to see just how easy it is to schedule and host a Google Meet:

- How to Schedule a Google Meet: https://youtu.be/3wFqRbNdWjA (60 seconds)
- How to Be a Pro at Google Meets: https://youtu.be/iKhTHVaerLI (90 seconds)
- Troubleshooting Sound/Video Issues: https://youtu.be/Fl7ohlSImJU (180 seconds)

It's impossible to replace the experience of mingling in person, but we shouldn't assume or conclude that there's nothing more we can do during a pandemic.

chapter 4
GOOGLE MEETS FOR COVID CHURCHES

Google Meets makes it easy (and free) to connect anytime.

Why Not Zoom?

Upon introducing this idea to my national group of Women's Ministry Leaders, I learned that many churches and small groups had, indeed, given up on Zoom because of an "intimidation factor."

If you're familiar and comfortable with Zoom, it may be unfathomable to realize people are afraid to use it. But it's a fact.

- Downloading can be an issue.
- Technology and connection problems may have made them feel exposed or unsure of themselves.
- There are so many reasons people get scared off Zoom.

On the other hand, Google Meets can be mastered in just sixty seconds. Computer phobic attendees have found that it is truly simple enough to be doable, and here's why:

21

- No passwords.
- Nothing to download.
- No Google or Gmail account required to attend.
- No bells and whistles, just...
- One click, on one link, and they're in.

chapter 5
BRING 'EM B.A.C.
(BEFORE & AFTER CHURCH)

A lot of churches haven't yet progressed to the point of providing interactive options for saints watching from home.

If that's you, it's completely understandable: You've been busy reopening and focusing on your returning on-premise attendees.

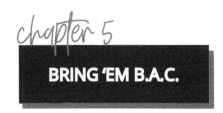

chapter 5
BRING 'EM B.A.C.

This resource introduces the idea of establishing Before & After Church (BAC) online meeting rooms using the simple platform of Google Meets.

Prior to 2020, faithful churchgoers would never have felt comfortable or even considered church hopping or disappearing for months at a time.

Never has there been such a wide variety of legitimate options for church attendance on Sunday mornings.

As you take another look at the chart on the following page, you'll notice the spaces where growth potential lies.

Bottom Line: Your folks at home are just trying to survive this unprecedented and prolonged isolation, too.

COPYRIGHT 2020 © WWW.MARNIE.COM

chapter 5
BRING 'EM B.A.C.

ON PREMISE	ONLINE
Leave the house with anticipation.	Boot up the computer.
Arrive, park, walk and greet as you go.	**HOST BEFORE CHURCH FOYER-STYLE CHAT ROOMS**
Greet and be greeted in the foyer.	
Find a seat and converse with neighbors.	
Enjoy the service, get lost in the Spirit, singing loudly, and be present in the moment.	Watch and do your best to sing along despite feeling self-conscious. Try to stay focused while being distracted by other online options.
Receive prayer at the altar if needed.	**HOST AFTER CHURCH ENGAGEMENT GROUPS**
Greet others on your way out.	
Arrive home two or more hours later or go out for lunch with friends.	Begin to do something else one minute later.

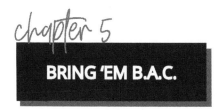

BRING 'EM B.A.C.

Reactivate Your Stranded Leaders

While every congregant has been affected by shutdowns, your leaders have been uniquely affected. Just because they're home doesn't mean they've stopped being who Christ created them to be.

Leaders exist to serve and are eager to be useful. They yearn for responsibility and long to be recognized for their God-given gifts and talents.

Make a list of names, including every person with leadership skills who is still at home who might be interested in hosting a meeting room, or taking charge of launching, or coordinating the entire BAC initiative.

chapter 6
TYPES OF ONLINE OPPORTUNITIES TO OFFER

The essential structure of your BAC (Before & After Church) meetings includes:

- Foyer-style meeting rooms before church for casual conversations.
- Foyer-style meeting rooms after church PLUS

chapter 6
TYPES OF ONLINE OPPORTUNITIES TO OFFER

- "Deeper Dive" meeting rooms after church where small groups can discuss aspects of the sermon based on sermon notes and interaction questions provided by the pastor.

While Google allows up to 100 people per meeting room, for our purposes, the smaller the group, the better for interaction. An online room of twelve people or less is ideal, however, rooms with two to four participants for casual conversation and catching up will certainly boost morale.

In addition to BAC (Before and After Church) meetups, other ideas could include:

- Impromptu face-to-face online chats
- Parties, showers, celebrations
- Small group Bible studies, and more.

Let's lower the bar, remove obstacles, and equip every saint to host and participate in online meetings. As church leaders, we need to care for

Chapter 6
TYPES OF ONLINE OPPORTUNITIES TO OFFER

our attendees while giving them a practical way to continue to invite guests.

What Facebook's FaceTime did for grandparents, Google Meets can do for the church. Once your congregation is equipped, there's no stopping them.

Imagine if the parents of adult children could invite their unchurched kids from near and far to join them for online church via a private meet-up BAC room. How great would that be?

The myriad potential uses and variations for Google Meets are beyond the scope of this resource, but there's one thing we can know: We can get the ball rolling and start bringing 'em BAC!

chapter 7

30-SECONDS TO SUCCESS

Did you know that Google Meets can be scheduled in less than 30-seconds? It's possible your people will want to schedule follow-up, one-on-one, get-togethers *even before they leave* their BAC room. (i.e. – Let's eat lunch together while we further discuss this idea.)

chapter 7
30-SECONDS TO SUCCESS

Here's a simple formula for your success.

S — **Start by teaching your whole church how to use Google Meets.**

While your online church will be most affected by the addition of the BAC rooms, invite your entire church to learn how to host these rooms. Your goal is inclusion-one church body that maintains a sense of oneness versus feelings of alienation. Gift *everyone* with the same tool and training, all at the same time.

U — **Utilize your at-home leaders to host your meetups.**

Avoid the blind spot of "out of sight, out of mind." Your leaders at home are praying for opportunities to serve. They wonder if God has put them on

chapter 7
30-SECONDS TO SUCCESS

the backburner or a shelf to gather dust. They're hoping you haven't forgotten them and all they have to offer. Identify your leaders and invite them to host rooms and/or manage this ministry.

C Capture the hearts of your lonely, stuck-at-home church.

BAC rooms offer an amazingly doable interim resource for immediately communicating your love, inclusion, and compassion for your saints at home.

C Celebrate Before & After Church, plus any livestreamed event.

What other events do you livestream? Consider adding BAC rooms for them as well. Do what is feasible for you. Maybe consider adding a few

chapter 7
30-SECONDS TO SUCCESS

computers around the foyer for walk-by greetings. Get creative! Remember, people need to interact. Give them a reason to get out of their sweatpants and jammies.

E Express your joy at the thought of attendees gathering often.

Avoid getting territorial. Gift this skill set to your entire congregation and give them your blessing to use it in any way that makes sense to them. Then stand back and watch how God blesses your faithfulness.

S Supply them with video tutorials as well as a tech-support team.

In addition to the three tutorial videos linked to in Chapter 4, establish your own BAC tech-support team. Who do you know that is stuck at home

chapter 7

30-SECONDS TO SUCCESS

with the skill set to help non-techy attendees get connected? Make an effort to recruit them. Invite them to set up a "BAC tech room" Google Meet link where people can come for further assistance.

S   Stand back and watch God grow your overall church attendance.

When you tap into your at-home congregation by inviting them to attend, interact, participate, and serve, you'll find that they'll be more inclined to invite their friends and neighbors.

Consider how God will use this win-win-win situation to bring 'em BAC and train more volunteers, all the while motivating and equipping every participant to help grow God's church.

chapter 8
LOOKING BEHIND TO PLAN AHEAD

Have you ever felt fearful about your future? Have you ever missed a plane? Maybe you've been excluded from a party or group.

Losses, real or imagined, feel bad. The losses incurred in 2020 will go down in history.

chapter 8
LOOKING BEHIND TO PLAN AHEAD

I'd like to share a memory I feel will help you take action amidst the chaos instead of waiting until things calm down. It's the story of the 1997 Red River Valley Flood.

- In March, the valley experienced freezing rain that devastated trees and power lines for miles.
- The spring thaw resulted in flooding at levels of destruction unheard of in over 100 years.
- During the flood, power surges in downtown, high-rise buildings started fires that couldn't be put out due to flood waters keeping fire fighters away. What the floods didn't destroy, the fires did.
- Post-flood, tornadoes bombarded the area due to the extra moisture in the atmosphere.

The coronavirus pandemic is a season like that, but instead of a wreaking havoc in a region or single community, this disaster is affecting the entire world.

chapter 8
LOOKING BEHIND TO PLAN AHEAD

It's one disaster after another heartbreaking disaster.

Dealing with crushing circumstances, we have unintentionally "shunned" our at-home saints. This was not done deliberately, but having seen it now, we need to address the inequities quickly and effectively lest they further corrode the shorelines of our churches.

Reach out! Revive, bolster and shore up both your on-premise and online congregations for the potential troubles yet to come. Here's how:

- Prayerfully consider what God is calling YOUR church to do.
- Recognize the indomitable spirits that exist in your stranded-at-home church family.
- Engage people by asking them to volunteer, and then train them.
- Prepare your entire congregation to capture every potential connection opportunity.

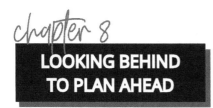

LOOKING BEHIND TO PLAN AHEAD

- Honor your saints at home by connecting with them in a NEW way. Do not let anyone suffer alone while waiting for a break in the bad news.

Your invisible army is about to become your front-line heroes in this ongoing war against the long-term ramifications of COVID-19 and its fall-out.

Those at home await a call from someone-anyone who will invite them to re-engage.

appendix I

THE 5WS

The first thing your Google Meet leaders will need is a clear set of directions. They can't say "YES!" until they understand your goals, how to utilize Google Meets, and most importantly, how to meet *your* expectations.

Nobody wants to fail.

Your first task is to write up your church's rendition of a COVID BAC plan. Who? What? When? Where? Why?

Next, share your plan, plus a copy of this resource, with every potential leader for their prayerful consideration.

Here's an example of a 5W document:

BRING 'EM B.A.C.
(BEFORE & AFTER CHURCH)

Who?
We are enlisting at-home attendees to coordinate a new, online ministry, hosting Before and After Church meeting rooms. We need room hosts, a ministry coordinator, and a technical support team.

What?
Online meeting rooms will provide the opportunity for foyer-style, casual conversations as well as after church small group rooms for those who want to discuss the sermon.

When?
Online Before & After Church meeting rooms will take place on Sundays and for other live-streamed church

---

COPYRIGHT 2020 © WWW.MARNIE.COM

THE 5WS

events. In addition, we are encouraging people to host meetings for any reason, any time, on their own.

Where?

Due to its simplicity, we'll be using Google Meets. Meeting rooms will be scheduled and posted in advance along with their respective online links. Hosts will greet people as they join and help them find their way around the chat features.

Why?

Our saints at home are ready to do more than WATCH church. They're ready for action, engagement, and interaction. Some crave responsibility and we're excited to step up and offer it to them with confidence.

COPYRIGHT 2020 © WWW.MARNIE.COM

appendix II
INSIGHTS FROM SUCCESSFUL ROOM HOSTS

Our test groups of Women's Ministry Leaders unearthed some strategic treasures to help simplify and maximize your BAC room engagements.

1. Invitations should always include Google Meet room addresses (i.e. - meet.google.com/qsa-gjdb-xdg) as well as the link to the tech support room. It is possible to

appendix II
INSIGHTS FROM SUCCESSFUL ROOM HOSTS

use the same rooms both before and after church. You can even use the same links from week to week.

2. Encourage your room hosts to spend no more than 30 seconds trying to help someone who's having connection issues. Instead, send them over to the tech support room where they can get all the help they need before coming back. This provides a smooth, non-threatening experience for all attendees.

3. Adopt the 5:3 Method

    a. Use the first five minutes for meet and greet. Trying to start right on time is a mistake.

    b. Use the next three minutes to provide a seamless "invisible tutorial" of how the room will be used. This shouldn't feel like a tutorial, but more like a quick check of the system.

        i. Ask someone, by name, to "test" their microphone. Tell them where to look for it each week. The goal

appendix II
INSIGHTS FROM SUCCESSFUL ROOM HOSTS

is that every new guest gets a tutorial without feeling singled out or intimidated.

ii. Ask someone else, by name, to "test" the chat area by explaining exactly where it is. Have them text you all the message HELLO (or whatever).

iii. Tell everyone they can mute themselves or go "off-camera" anytime using the buttons at the bottom center of their screen.

4. If guests want to "room hop" or leave to attend the main service, have them completely exit (or "x" out) instead of keeping the screens active in several rooms. This will prevent unnecessary feedback issues.

5. Room hosts have the option to remove a guest (i.e. – if they forget to "x" out).

6. When anyone exits the room, their chat area is cleared. If you, as the host, want to retain

appendix II
INSIGHTS FROM SUCCESSFUL ROOM HOSTS

your chat notes, mute yourself before you move to a new tab. Keep the Google Meet window open. Come and go as desired.

7. As host, you can ask individuals to mute themselves, or you can mute them. You cannot unmute them, but they can unmute themselves at any time.

8. Use the "pin" option to bring someone to center screen if you want to see them more clearly. Attendees can PIN each other, and it's all private. No one can see who's pinning whom.

9. You may share your screen using the "Present Now" option. Practice this in advance if you want to use it during a live meet. For example, if you'd like to share something on the desktop such as scripture verse or photo, use this feature.

10. It's okay for the host to leave before the last person. Just politely excuse yourself and let the remaining attendees carry on. After all, it's about increasing engagement and not about you.

ABOUT THE AUTHOR

Marnie Swedberg is a leadership mentor to over 15,000 leaders from 35 countries, providing Courage & Clarity consulting, coaching, collaborations and conference keynotes around the world.

Her programs and resources provide perspective transforming Biblical success principles, deep spiritual healing and hope to women everywhere.

She is the author of 13 books, host of a #1 ranked and featured Blog Talk Radio Show and the founder/director of WomenSpeakers.com, the largest directory of its kind in the world.

Learn more at www.Marnie.com.

Connect with Marnie

YouTube:
www.youtube.com/c/GodlyWomenWorldwide

Facebook:
https://www.facebook.com/SpeakerMarnie

Twitter:
https://twitter.com/MentorMarnie

LinkedIn:
https://www.linkedin.com/in/marnieswedberg

Pinterest:
https://www.pinterest.com/mentormarnie/

Instagram:
https://www.instagram.com/mentormarnie/

BlogTalkRadio:
www.blogtalkradio.com/marniesfriends

Amazon:
https://amzn.to/2JJoyun

Made in the USA
Columbia, SC
25 June 2025